When Penguins
CROSS THE ICE

THE EMPEROR PENGUIN MIGRATION

by Sharon Katz Cooper   illustrated by Tom Leonard

PICTURE WINDOW BOOKS
a capstone imprint

Thanks to our advisers for their expertise, research, and advice:

Gerald Kooyman, Research Professor
Scripps Institution of Oceanography, La Jolla, California

Terry Flaherty, PhD, Professor of English
Minnesota State University, Mankato

Editor: Jill Kalz
Designer: Lori Bye
Art Director: Nathan Gassman
Production Specialist: Laura Manthe
The illustrations in this book were created with acrylics.
Image Credit: Shutterstock: Volina, 3 (map)

Picture Window Books are published by Capstone,
1710 Roe Crest Drive, North Mankato, Minnesota 56003
www.capstoneyoungreaders.com

Library of Congress Cataloging-in-Publication Data
Katz Cooper, Sharon, author.
  When penguins cross the ice : the Emperor penguin migration / by
Sharon Katz Cooper ; illustrated by Tom Leonard.
      pages cm.—(Nonfiction picture books. Extraordinary migrations)
  Summary: "Follows a single Emperor penguin on its annual migration
journey"—Provided by publisher.
  Audience: K to grade 3.
  Includes bibliographical references and index.
  ISBN 978-1-4795-6078-3 (library binding)
  ISBN 978-1-4795-6106-3 (paper over board)
  ISBN 978-1-4795-6110-0 (eBook PDF)
1. Emperor penguin—Migration—Juvenile literature. 2. Emperor
penguin—Behavior—Juvenile literature. 3. Animal migration—Juvenile
literature. I. Leonard, Thomas, 1955– illustrator. II. Title. III. Title:
Emperor penguin migration.
  QL696.S473K38 2015
  598.47—dc23   2014024415

EDITOR'S NOTE: Antarctica and the
surrounding waters are home to more than 50
colonies of emperor penguins. Each year about
200,000 breeding pairs migrate from the sea.
Most travel only a few miles. But one small
group, the Pointe Géologie colony, travels a
long way. Its members may walk up to
70 miles (113 kilometers) across the ice. This
book tells the story of one of those penguins.

Printed in the United States of America in North Mankato, Minnesota.
102014   008482CGS15

Emperor penguins live in one of the coldest, darkest places on Earth—Antarctica. In winter, temperatures may drop to minus 40 degrees Fahrenheit (minus 40 degrees Celsius). Each year thousands of emperor penguins make an amazing journey across the ice. They leave the ocean's edge and travel to places with no food and very little warmth. Why is this migration so important to them?

ANTARCTICA

● emperor penguin breeding ground

0	500	1000	1500	2000 kilometers
0	316	632	948	1264 miles

Pointe Géologie

Splash! The emperor penguin dives into the water. It is February, the end of the Antarctic summer. A hard winter lies ahead. To prepare for it, the penguin fills himself up with fish and krill.

4

Days grow shorter. March arrives. It is time for the penguin to leave the sea.

A long line of male and female emperor penguins stretches across the ice. He joins them, marching single-file. Sometimes he slides on his belly to save energy.

A few days later, the penguin reaches the breeding ground. Thousands more arrive soon. One of the female penguins catches his eye. The two get to know each other. After about one month, they mate.

In late May the female lays one egg. The egg is why the penguins have traveled so far. Carefully the male takes the egg from the female. This is a big moment. If the egg sits too long on the icy ground, the chick inside the shell will die.

The male penguin covers the egg with his brood pouch. Once the egg is safe, his mate heads back to the open ocean. The journey is long, but she must go. There is no way to get food at the breeding ground. For about two months, the mother penguin will eat all she can. Then she will return to help raise her chick.

The male penguin stays behind. He and the other males stand together with their eggs on their feet. They take turns being on the outside of the group, where it's coldest. Through the darkest and windiest winter days, they huddle to keep the eggs warm. They eat nothing at all.

Peck, peck! Crack! After about 70 days, the egg hatches. Out wiggles a hungry baby penguin!

Even though the father penguin has not eaten for nearly four months, his body does something amazing. It makes crop milk. The special milk is made inside the father penguin's throat and fed to the chick by mouth.

In August the mother penguin returns.
Thousands of other penguins are already there.
To find her mate, she calls out. He calls back.
Right away the mother penguin takes over
feeding the chick. She gives it partly eaten food
from her stomach.

Now, at last, the father penguin can head to
the sea to fill his own stomach!

The mother and father penguins take turns
caring for their chick. Once it's about 50 days old,
the chick can be left alone for a time. It huddles
together with other chicks in a crèche while its
parents search for food.

December comes, and so does summer! A lot of the ice by the ocean's edge melts. The distance from the breeding ground to open water shrinks.

The parent penguins return to the ocean. Their young are ready to be on their own. In a few weeks, they too will dive into the sea.

Emperor Penguin Fast Facts

Scientific name: *Aptenodytes forsteri*

Height: about 39 inches (99 centimeters) tall

Weight: 49–99 pounds (22–45 kilograms)

Life span: 15–20 years

Home: spends about three-fourths of its life in the water

Egg weight (average): 1 pound (454 grams)

Diet: fish, crustaceans, krill, squid

Predators: leopard seals, petrels, skuas

Breath control: can stay underwater nearly 28 minutes

Migration: from a few miles to 70 miles (113 kilometers) each way

Group name: colony

Dive Deeper

1. Why is it important for thousands of emperor penguins to journey across the ice each year?

2. Explain the steps the male emperor penguin takes to keep his egg (and later, his newly hatched chick) safe.

3. What is the purpose of a brood pouch?

Glossary

breeding ground—the place where penguins go to find mates and raise their chicks

brood pouch—a flap of feather-covered skin that male penguins use to warm and protect their eggs and chicks

chick—a young bird

colony—a large group of animals that live together in the same area

crèche (KRESH)—a group or cluster of chicks

krill—a small, shrimplike animal

mate—to join together to produce young; a mate is also the male or female partner of a pair of animals

migration—the movement from one area to another on a regular basis, usually to find food or to produce young

predator—an animal that hunts other animals for food

Read More

Bodden, Valerie. *Penguins.* Amazing Animals. Mankato, Minn.: Creative Education, 2010.

Landau, Elaine. *Emperor Penguins: Animals of the Snow and Ice.* Animals of the Snow and Ice. Berkeley Heights, N.J.: Enslow Elementary, 2011.

Lock, Deborah. *Emperor Penguins.* DK Readers. Level 2, Beginning to Read Alone. London; New York: DK Publishing, 2011.

Molnar, Michael. *Emperor Penguins.* Life Cycles of Marine Animals. Mankato, Minn.: Smart Apple Media, 2012.

Index

About the Author

Sharon Katz Cooper is a science educator and freelance writer who specializes in science and social studies topics. She has written more than 25 books for children, including a series called Horrible Habitats, which was recommended by the National Science Teachers Association (NSTA). She is based in Pittsburgh, Penn., where she lives with her husband and three boys, Reuven, Judah, and Yaron.

About the Illustrator

Tom Leonard has been a freelance illustrator for more than 20 years. A graduate of the Philadelphia College of Art (now called the University of the Arts) with a degree in Illustration, he has worked for numerous publications throughout his career, including *Psychology Today*, *Reader's Digest*, *International Wildlife*, and *Science Digest*. Since 1993 he has focused on children's books, usually with a view toward nature. Tom has had several shows throughout Philadelphia, and his work has appeared in the *Graphis Annual* and the *Society of Illustrators*. Tom teaches at the University of the Arts and also teaches summers at Fleisher Art Memorial, where he has exhibited his work on several occasions. Tom lives in South Philadelphia with his wife, Rose.

LOOK FOR ALL THE BOOKS IN THE SERIES:

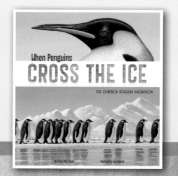

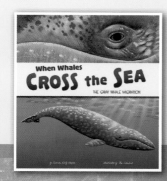